# MEDITERRANEAN
# MEAL PREP

### Complete Beginner's Guide to
### Save Time and Eat Healthier with
### Batch Cooking for The Mediterranean Diet

## ELIZABETH WELLS

# TABLE OF CONTENTS

## Free Bonus:
## The Best Foods To Eat On A Ketogenic Diet

Discover the best foods to eat on a ketogenic diet. You'll learn the different food groups that you should eat to follow the keto diet correctly and start improving your health right now.

Go to **www.eepurl.com/cUqOlH** to download the guide for free.

# Introduction

I am so glad you took time out of your busy schedule to download your copy of Mediterranean Meal Prep: Complete Beginner's Guide To Save Time And Eat Healthier With Batch Cooking For The Mediterranean Diet. Thank you for doing so.

You will discover how important planning is when you visit the grocery store and
are tempted by all of the food that can be prepared quickly. The only way to fight the urge is to plan ahead and store essential products until you need them.

Keep the menu preparation plans rolling, and you will get spoiled by how simple it is to maintain a healthy diet and subsequently, a healthy lifestyle. The meal prep plan will work whether you are prepping for four days or a week. Choose a day when you don't have any plans and get tossing and prepare the meals you desire for your family.

The following chapters will also discuss a specific diet plan that has been used in countries such as Spain, Greece, and Italy as well as other Mediterranean locations dating back to the 1960s. It was discovered when researchers noticed these individuals were much healthier when compared to the Americans, and that Mediterranean people also had such a low risk of so many diseases that could be deadly.

You can lose and maintain a healthy weight and discover a sustainable way to reduce any disease-causing inflammation. The fortunate part of the diet plan (also called the Med Diet) is that you don't have to travel to an exotic country to enjoy the cuisine. You can prepare these meals using tools and appliances in your kitchen. You will be using foods stocked in your cupboards.

You will also learn how to follow the new Mediterranean diet plan and the ways it will most benefit your health. By following the diet plan, you will be consuming an abundance of olive oil, fruits, legumes, vegetables, and whole grains. The diet features lean choices of protein including fish and poultry instead of red meats which contain more saturated fat (can be eaten occasionally). You can also consume red wine moderately.

Each of the recipes has been planned explicitly for the Mediterranean diet to ensure you are receiving the right balance of each of the essential nutrients. Some of the recipe ingredients may be listed in grams, and you will need to use a conversion chart. When you see one, simply use the chart to convert to English measurements.

You will notice throughout the book that the recipes will mention 'divided.' Essentially, this means you will use the ingredient in more than one place in the recipe. You will also discover EVOO as an abbreviation for extra-virgin olive oil which is a very important ingredient for the Mediterranean way of living. Each of the recipes has a number for your convenience.

There are plenty of books offered on this subject in today's market, thanks again for choosing this one! Every effort was made to ensure that it is full of as much useful information as possible. Please enjoy!

Let's Begin!

# Chapter 1:
## Meal Prep 101

The concept of meal preparation is to provide healthy plant-based meals for your family for more than two days or in some cases at least overnight. Think of it as you could be packing a meal for breakfast, lunch or dinner that can be readily available by simply opening the refrigerator or freezer.

Each of the meals provided will show you how to proceed with ease. You can increase or decrease the amounts prepared to meet your family's needs. Once you have a routine the process will be so easy you will wonder where it has been when not in your kitchen.

### Getting Started with Meal Prep

One of the key elements to make the plan effective is to make it fun. Play some of your favorite music or linger over a talk show; anything to get you motivated!

Take an active inventory of the pantry and other food storage areas.

Choose the Menu: Gather your favorite recipes or try some new ones in your new meal prep book.

### Choose a Preparation Day In Advance:

Get everyone involved because the job will be much easier and even enjoyable. Decide as a team what you want to eat for the coming week. Try to choose a menu that has many of the same items or ones that can be saved for one in the next preparation batch. You want to prepare enough to last until the end of the week. You can choose several ways.

All of the prep doesn't have to be done on the same day if you have a plan. Use the prepared foods - that will not last as long as others – first. It will be much simpler once you have established a workable routine. When you start running out of necessary meal items, just find another recipe and prep with the foods you have left.

## Plan Shopping & Meal Planning Ahead of Time:

You will need to understand the shelf life of different foods. It is important to stock up on the items that are non-perishable about once each month. Fresh produce may require a bi-weekly trip. Other food items should be purchased according to your menu plan for the week. The key is to keep a 'watchful eye' on the expiration dates. It is imperative to date and mark every food item prepared in advance at storage time.

Place fruits and other items that may need some ripening before using on the countertop to finish the process at room temperature. When the desired ripeness level is reached simply place it in the refrigerator or use it. You can freeze items, but many studies have indicated that foods are lower in nutrients when frozen and thawed.

## The Best Products for Easy Prep

- Mason Jars – Pint or quart sized
- Rubbermaid Stackable or Glad Containers
- Ziploc-type freezer bags
- Glass containers with tight-fitting lids
- Metal containers with sealable lids

## The Standard for Containers

- Freezer Safe
- Microwavable
- BPA Free
- Reusable
- Stackable

Be sure to label each one with the date and contents.

## Layer and Label the Containers Correctly

You can ruin your entire process of meal prep if you don't keep your jars and containers properly layered. You want to begin with the thick/harder veggies such as cabbage and carrots, then your softer ones such as beans or chickpeas. Lastly, you want to add the greens or nuts on top. However, some recipes may have a different method, just follow the recipe because there is a reason for layering in the manner shown.

Also, place a sticker on the chosen container, so you are sure to rotate your inventory and prevent spoilage of your meal prepped items. Don't place it in your memory or the 'sniff test' to decide whether the food is still edible.

All you need to do is label with the 'use by' date or the day of preparation – whichever is the easiest for you to remember; just remain consistent. This is essential whether you choose to use a freezer bag, aluminum pan, glass pan, or other containers. Bulk freezing is a great way to stay in line but be sure to rotate the stock just like it's done in the supermarket.

## Always Use Fresh Ingredients

Make your list and go to the market with a prepared grocery list of the bowls/jars you want to prepare for the week. Do your meal prep the following day to ensure the freshness is maintained.

## How to Go the Cheapest Route – Meal Prep

Here is a quick example of how easy the process can be with a little planning.

## The Steps:

- Prep the smoothies in a container or bag.
- Cook Quinoa and Rice.
- Chop all veggies, coat in oil, salt, and bake.
- Portion the Containers.
- Done!

## Use the Slow Cooker:

If you have a slow cooker, it is the best way to serve a mouth-watering meal without a lot of extra work. You just have to add all of the fixings into the cooker and let it go. You can prepare the evening before and refrigerate until the morning. Turn it on when you go out of the door for a tasty meal when you learn. Now that is easy prep!

## Freezer Prepped Items:

Many of the items in your new book will allow you to freeze items until you have a need for them. If you are on a tight schedule, it is great to know all you have to do is go home and prepare an 'emergency' meal. It will give you one less thing to worry about during your day.

This is particularly true if you have problems in humid areas. Your bread and nuts cannot take the humidity, making the freezer a superb option to save not only money but the time it takes to prepare the items.

## Prepare a Grocery List:

The list is an important part of your meal preparation process:

- **Save Money**: If you are like many other shoppers, the 'blue light specials' in the store are a tempting factor. So, unless you have a need for the special purchase, it may be best if left on the grocery shelf. You will not be purchasing expensive items you don't really need. Your bank account will appreciate your diligence.

- **Stick to the Diet Plan**: You have made all of the right steps – so far. Don't let the temptations take over. That is the benefit of the list. You won't walk aimlessly around the store seeking what you need; you already have the essential items in your list. There's nothing more frustrating than to begin your meal prep to discover you don't have the ingredients you need. Save the time, energy, and fuel to make an unplanned grocery run since it will take away from the task at hand – your meal prep.

## Food Preparation Safety

The safety of you and your family may depend on your education on how to store your food items. Common sense will take you part of the way, but this list will help you stay safe while handling your items during prep.

1.  Wash your hands, all utensils, and your prep spaces after touching any raw meats.

2.  Keep raw meats away from other food ingredients.

3.  Store raw meats in the lowest section of the refrigerator. Even if the food is in a closed container, don't take the chance of any spillage.

4.  Keep a watchful eye on the 'use by' dates on the foods. This rule is particularly true of dairy and meat items. Produce is more adaptable, especially if it is cooked and not consumed in its raw state.

5.  For veggies and fruit, be sure to keep all surfaces germ-free just as you did with meats. It is less common to have issues from bacteria, but pesticides could be on the veggies before they are washed.

6.  Wash all fruit and veggies thoroughly before you begin to prep. The raw items should be kept away from other foods such as nuts and prepped salads that cannot be cleaned

7.  Be sure to cook items you are cooking for your prep entirely to avoid any contamination.

8.   Be sure to check guidelines for reheating your food inventory.

9.   Do not refreeze meat that has been defrosted. After it is defrosted, it must be used within 24 hours.

10.  Be sure to store meat separately if you plan on keeping it in the freezer for some time; even cooked meats.

11.  Once the food is prepared, cool quickly, and place in a sealed container, and place it in the refrigerator or freezer immediately.

## Cooked Food Guidelines

Using a food thermometer will help you safely prepare food. These guidelines are provided by the USDA for quality standards of safe cooking.

- Poultry – 165°F
- Ground Meats - 160°F – Pork, beef, veal, lamb, etc.
- Red Meats – 145°F – Lamb, beef, veal, pork, etc.

## Cool Foods Rapidly:

It is important to prevent bacterial growth by maintaining the storage temperature at 40°F or below. When preparing your foods, use shallow containers if it is a large recipe. For example, a large pot of soup will take a great deal of time to cool. Divide it into smaller containers for a faster cooling process.

The same idea works for roasted meats and similar items. Slice it up the way you will be using it – sliced or diced – and place it into a closed container as soon as it is cool. Wing and leg portions of the meat will be okay left whole.

## Tightly Cover – Store & Thaw the Food Safely

Use one of the storage methods described in this book for safe food storage. They will help retain the food's moisture and nutrients as well as keeping out any harmful bacteria. Immediately freeze or refrigerate the wrapped items for rapid cooling and safety.

Many foods can be stored in the freezer for 3-4 months and in the refrigerator for 3-4 days. Keep in mind that frozen products can lose moisture if frozen for longer times.

To safely thaw the foods, you can use a cold-water soak, the refrigerator, or microwave. Use caution if using the water method and make sure there are no holes in the container where foreign substances could reach the food.

If you use the microwave, the fastest method, be sure the heat reaches a continuous 165°F when measured with a food thermometer. If you thaw too much product, at this time, you *can* refreeze the food.

The refrigerator is the best method because the frozen items will remain at a more constant temperature. Be sure to use the items right away and never refreeze them.

# Chapter 2:
## The Mediterranean Lifestyle

### History of the Traditional Origins of the Mediterranean Diet

During the 1960s many traditional foods became popular originating points in Crete, Greece, and Southern Italy as the baseline for many menu plans. American researchers began to detect how these people had remained so much healthier in comparison to the people living in the United States.

The first to associate with the Mediterranean diet was *The Seven Countries Study* which began in 1957 and has lasted for decades. The study involved Finland, Yugoslavia, the Netherlands, Japan, Italy, Greece and the United States. The initial enrollment involved 12,000 healthy middle-aged men. Ancel Keys, the main investigator, discovered the seven countries had the lowest cardiovascular disease rates, apparently because of diet.

Many of the standard American diets are focused on refined carbohydrates, fried or fast foods and many others which contain high levels of saturated or trans fats, as well as sodium. These plans lead to deficiencies in minerals, vitamins, and fiber. Now, you see the difference.

### Benefits of the Plan

These are just a few of the ways the Mediterranean diet plan can provide you with a healthier lifestyle:

*Essential Nutrients are Consumed:* You probably wonder how all of this is possible with high fat in the diet. You are less likely to be hungry with protein, fiber, and healthy fats entering your body. The veggies will make up the volume of the meals. These types of foods will not cause a spike in blood sugar, resulting in hunger in an hour or so. You can make it through the day without all of the extra snacks.

*Improved Weight Loss:* Individuals on the Mediterranean diet plan lost over three times more weight than those on other plans as stated by a New England Journal of Medicine.

*Helps to Prevent Heart Attacks:* The reduced level of oxidized low-density lipoprotein (LDL) cholesterol is evident with the plan.

*Helps to Prevent Strokes and Alzheimer's Disease:* The reduction of blood sugar levels and general blood vessel health is improved.

*Improved Moods:* Over 15,000 individuals were studied in Spain and found the amounts of omega-3 fatty acids contributed to a lower risk of developing depression.

*The Plan Helps Keep Your Body Agile:* Muscle weakness and other frailty signs are reduced by as much as 70 % for those who followed the plan.

*Type 2 Diabetes:* There is better control of sugar levels/blood glucose

*Premature Death:* Over 1.5 million healthy adults have been associated with living a fuller life on the med diet plan. That calculates to a 20% reduced risk of death at any age.

## Tips of How to Achieve the Benefits

Adapting to a strict Mediterranean diet plan is best described as taking advantage of the methods used in a food pyramid of sorts. The following lists will provide essential information on how to balance the plan. These are those guidelines:

*Daily Goals*:

- Olive Oil: The main added lipid
- Dairy Products: Two servings
- Fruit: Three servings
- Veggies: Six servings
- Non-refined cereals and Similar Products: Eight Servings: This group includes brown rice, as well as whole grain pasta and bread.

*Weekly Goals*:

- Fish: Five to six servings
- Poultry: Four servings
- Nuts, olives, pulses: Three to four servings
- Eggs: Three servings
- Potatoes: Three servings
- Sweets: Three servings

*Monthly Goals*:

- Four servings of red meat

Add some physical activity to the combination and drink plenty of water. Replace some of your salt intake with herbs such as thyme, basil, and oregano.

## Basics of the Mediterranean Diet Plan

The basis of the diet calls for plant foods which are moderately low in animal foodstuffs. On the flip side, it is advisable to consume fish or seafood for at least two days each week. You will want to consume plenty of water, and one glass of red wine daily is admissible. Tea and coffee are okay, but you should avoid sweeteners.

## What You Should Eat

- Fruits: Dates, grapes, strawberries, oranges, apples, bananas, pears, peaches, melons, etc.
- Seeds and Nuts: Macadamia nuts, cashews, almonds, walnuts, pumpkin seeds, hazelnuts, sunflower seeds, etc.

- Dairy: Greek yogurt, cheese, yogurt
- Eggs: Duck, chicken, quail
- Healthy Fats: Olives, extra-virgin olive oil, avocado oil, and avocados
- Poultry: Turkey, duck, chicken
- Whole Grains: Brown rice, whole oats, barley, rye, whole wheat, buckwheat, corn, whole grain pasta, and whole grain bread, etc.
- Spices and Herbs: Cinnamon, garlic, mint, basil, sage, rosemary, pepper, nutmeg, etc.
- Seafood and Fish: Tuna, salmon, trout, sardines, shrimp mackerel, oysters, shrimp, crab, clams, mussels, etc.
- Vegetables: Kale, broccoli, tomatoes, carrots, cauliflower, spinach, onions, cucumbers, Brussels sprouts
- Legumes: Lentils, peas, beans, chickpeas, peanuts, pulses, etc.
- Tubers: Sweet potatoes, potatoes, yams, turnips, etc.

*Note*: Many of the Mediterranean Diet recipes call for olive oil; you will use the extra-virgin type if it is not specified.

## Eat These in Moderation

- Eggs
- Poultry
- Cheese
- Yogurt

*Note:* You can eat these food products but use in small amounts in your meals.

**Rarely Eat**: Red Meat

## Avoid These Foods

- Added Sugars: Ice cream, candy, soda, table sugar
- Sugar-Sweetened Beverages: Avoid juices high in sugar
- Refined Grains: Pasta made with refined wheat, white bread
- Processed Meat: Hot dogs, processed sausages, etc.
- Trans fats: Margarine and other processed foods
- Refined Oils: Canola, cottonseed, soybean, and others

- Higher Processed Foods: Any foods marked 'diet,' 'low-fat,' or factory produced

## Why Consider Switching to Olive Oil?

The monosaturated fat which is found in olive oil is a fat that can help reduce low-density lipoprotein cholesterol (LDL-C) or as you may know it - the bad cholesterol. The oil has become the traditional fat worldwide with some of the healthiest populations. A great deal of research has been provided showing the oil as a huge plus towards lowering the risk of heart disease since it contains so many antioxidants and fatty acids.

You will still need to pay close attention when purchasing olive oil because it may have been extracted from the olives using chemicals or possible diluted with other cheaper oils, such as canola and soybean. You need to be aware of refined or light olive or regular oils.

The Mediterranean diet plan calls for the use of extra-virgin olive oil because it has been standardized for purity using natural methods and provides the sensory qualities of its excellent taste and smell. The oil is high in phenolic antioxidants which makes real olive oil beneficial.

These are some of the nutrients contained in extra-virgin olive oil based on 100 grams (about 3.4 ounces):

- Monosaturated Fat: 73% (the 18 carbon long oleic acid)
- Saturated Fat: 13.8%
- Omega-3: 0.76%
- Omega-6: 9.7%
- Vitamin E is 72% of the RDA
- Vitamin K is 75% of the RDA

*Note*: RDA stands for the recommended dietary allowance or the recommended daily allowance. It is the number of nutrients necessary daily for the maintenance of good health calculated by the Food and Nutrition Board of the National Research Council.

Let's begin at Breakfast!

# Chapter 3:

## Tasty Breakfast & Brunch Choices

If you are a morning person – or not- you will surely find something in this segment to satisfy those early morning to mid-day hunger pains.

### Breakfast Quinoa with Dates & Apricots

Total Time: 30 min.
Servings: 4-6

### Ingredients:

1 c. quinoa
¼ c. chopped raw almonds
5 dried apricots
2 dried pitted dates
2 tbsp. honey
1 t. of each:
- Ground cinnamon
- Sea salt
- Vanilla extract

2 c. milk

### How to Prepare:

1. Finely chop the dates and apricots.
2. Using medium heat, toast the almonds three to five minutes in a skillet. Set aside.

3. Heat the quinoa, salt, and cinnamon using medium heat until warm. Pour in the milk.

4. When the mixture boils, lower the heat, and place a lid on the pan and continue cooking slowly for approximately 15 minutes.

5. Pour in the honey, vanilla, apricots, dates, and ½ of the almonds.

6. Garnish with the rest of the almonds for a tasty treat.

## Prepping Details:

1. Prepare the quinoa just as you did in steps 1-4. Let the mixture cool. You can pour it into individual servings or store it in a glass bowl until ready to eat.

2. When ready to have your meal, warm it up and add the splash of milk, honey, vanilla, dates, apricots and half of the almonds.

3. Garnish the top with the rest of the nuts.

## Breakfast Blueberries & Slow-Cooked Quinoa

Total Time: 4 hours 6 minutes
Servings: 4

### Ingredients:

1 c. dry quinoa
1 tbsp. honey
2 c. water
1 ¼ c. coconut milk – divided
1 t. vanilla extract
¼ c. sliced – toasted almonds
½ c. fresh fruit or blueberries

### How to Prepare:

1. Combine all of the fixings in the slow cooker – omitting the blueberries and almonds at this point.
2. Prepare using the high setting for 2 hrs. (low for 4 hrs.).
3. Once you are ready to serve, top it off with a splash of the milk, blueberries, and almonds. Peaches and other fruits are also tasty.

### Prepping Details:

1. You can prepare the ingredients in step 1 and 2.
2. Place the fixings in the refrigerator after it is cooled.
3. When you're ready to eat, just serve and enjoy.
4. You can also have the ingredients prepared (milk, nuts, and blueberries) if you want to use this as a to-go pack. (Place the rest of the ingredients in a closed container or Ziploc-type bag.)

# Cranberry Breakfast Muffins

Total Time: 25 minutes
Servings: 12

## Ingredients:

½ c. all-purpose flour
¼ c. sugar
1 ½ c. whole wheat flour
1 t. salt
3 t. baking powder
2 tbsp. honey
1 c. dried cranberries
1/3 c. olive oil
1 c. 2% milk
1 egg
Olive oil cooking spray

## How to Prepare:

1. Warm the oven to 400°F.
2. Sift or whisk each of the flours with the salt, sugar, and baking powder in a large mixing container.
3. Combine the eggs, milk, oil, and honey in another container.
4. Use a spoon to create a hole in the middle of the dry ingredients and blend in the wet fixings. Gently combine – don't overmix.
5. Use paper muffin cups or grease 12 muffin tin sections.
6. Bake 15-17 minutes and test with a toothpick. If the centers are clean when it's inserted; they're done.

## Prepping Details:

1. This is a super packer! The recipe provides you with 12 muffins.
2. Store them in the freezer.
3. When ready to eat; place in the microwave briefly. You can also store in the refrigerator.

## Polenta with Banana

Total Time: 10 minutes
Servings: 4

## Ingredients:

2 c. of each:
- Skim milk
- Water

1 c. quick-cooking/instant polenta
¼ t. salt
½ c. sliced banana
¼ c. honey
Optional: Greek yogurt

## How to Prepare:

1. Whisk the water, milk, and salt together in a saucepan using the med-low setting. Once boiling, continue to stir, so it doesn't scorch.
2. Pour in the polenta and stir. Switch to the low setting and continue cooking for another 2-5 min. Remove and add the honey.
3. Cool a minute. Add the banana slices and some Greek yogurt if you like it that way.

## Prepping Details:

1. Prepare the recipe ahead of time and place in the refrigerator. You can put it in individual dishes or in one; it's up to you. Do not add the banana.
2. When ready to eat, just pop it in the microwave until hot. Slice the banana and you are set.
3. It will store well in the refrigerator for 3-4 days using a closed glass container.

## Tofu Breakfast Scramble

Total Time: 1 hr. 25 min.
Servings: 8

### Ingredients:

5-6 c. or 1 ½ lb. sweet potatoes
1 tbsp. olive oil
½ t. salt
2 t. chili powder

### Ingredients for the Tofu Scramble:

½ red onion
1 block extra-firm tofu
2 bell peppers
2 c. asparagus
1 t. of each:
- Cumin
- Ground coriander

¼ t. pepper
½ t. salt

### How to Prepare:

1. Finely chop the onions and peppers. Also, chop the asparagus. Cube the potato into ½-inch cubes.
2. Program the oven temperature to 425°F.
3. Pour the oil into a dish and toss in the potatoes along with the salt and chili powder mixture. Arrange on a baking tin. Bake for 15 minutes.
4. Stir the mixture around a bit and continue baking about 15-20 more minutes.
5. Prepare the scramble while you wait. Use a potato masher and smash the tofu into small chunks.
6. Warm up oil in a skillet and saute the peppers, onions, and asparagus -about five minutes until softened. Toss in the coriander, cumin, salt, pepper, and tofu. Saute another two to

three minutes until incorporated.

## Prepping Details:

## Assemble the Bowls:

1. Equally, divide the scramble into the containers (6-8).
2. Store in the refrigerator for up to four days.

## To Serve:

1. Heat in the microwave on medium for one minute – or until warmed entirely.
2. Top it off with some Greek yogurt, cherry tomatoes, or avocado.

## Tuscan Veggie Frittata

Total Time: 34 minutes
Servings: 6

### Ingredients:

1 ½ c. chopped spinach
1/3 c. milk
6 eggs
½ c. of each:
- Chopped black olives
- Sundried tomatoes

¼ c. crumbled feta cheese
½ t. olive oil
1 t. Italian seasoning
Fresh basil
Also Needed: Deep pie plate or square baking pan

### How to Prepare:

1. Warm up the oven ahead of time to 400°F.
2. Measure out the oil into the chosen pan.
3. Whisk the eggs and milk. Toss in the olives, tomatoes, cheese, and Italian seasoning.
4. Top it off with a bit of feta and fresh basil.

### Prepping Details:

The four servings can be stored in a glass container in the refrigerator for several days. You can also slice and place it in foil to store in the refrigerator. The individual wrapper will allow you to grab and go.

**Oats**

## Coconut Ginger Overnight Oats

Total Time: 8 hr. – 5 min.
Servings: 1

### Ingredients for the Oats:

¼ - ½ c. coconut milk
¾ c. old-fashioned oats
¼ t. ground ginger
1 tbsp. agave syrup

### Ingredients for the Toppings:

2 tbsp. grated candied ginger
¼ c. raw, toasted coconut flakes

**Also Needed:** 4 (1) Pint Mason jars

### How to Prepare:

1. Make the Oats: Combine the oats with the ginger. In a small dish, combine the milk with the agave syrup. Use less milk if you prefer a thicker oat dish.
2. Pour the mixtures together and place in the refrigerator. Tightly secure the lid and refrigerate about 8 hours or overnight.

### Prepping Details:

1. At breakfast, simply top off the oatmeal with the coconut flakes and candied ginger.
2. Screw on the top and head off to work or eat immediately.
3. Note: Prepare as many servings in advance as you wish.

# Honey Walnut Overnight Oats

Total Time: 5 minutes (+) overnight for prep
Servings: 4

## Ingredients:

1 c. oats
3 ½ c. water
1 pinch of salt
½ t. vanilla extract
½ c. chopped walnuts
¼ c. of each:
- Honey
- Chopped pitted dates or raisins
- Milk

## How to Prepare:

1. Add a pinch of salt to the water and wait for it to boil.
2. Add the oats and stir. Turn off the heat.
3. Cover the pan and leave it out all night.

## Prepping Details:

1. When you want to serve breakfast, just turn on the stove and let the delicious oats get warm.
2. Stir in the raisins or dates with the honey.
3. Add the nuts and a splash of milk if you like it that way.

## Smoothies

### Strawberry Mango Smoothie with Greek Yogurt

Total Time: 10 min.
Servings: 4

### Ingredients:

½ c. soy/almond milk
1 c. of each:
- Frozen mango
- Greek yogurt
- Frozen strawberries

Optional: ¼ t. ground cinnamon

### How to Prepare:

1. Combine all of the fixings in a blender.
2. Pulse until creamy and blended thoroughly.

### Prepping Details:

1. You can create this delicious smoothie and store in the refrigerator. Be sure to use a glass jar with a lid.
2. It will be tasty for up to 3 days.

## Smoothies for 1

You can add as many as you like with the variations listed:

### Avocado Smoothie

### Ingredients:

3 celery stalks
½ avocado
1 lime
1 t. linseeds
Fresh mint leaves

### Prepping Details:

1. Store the fresh mint leaves in a separate Ziploc bag or another container.

## Beetroot Smoothie

## Ingredients:

2 t. minced ginger
1 boiled beetroot
1 tbsp. lemon juice
1 carrot
1 pear
1 apple

## Prepping Details:

1. Combine all of the fixings in a blender.
2. Add to individual glasses and store until you are ready to use.
3. Add a few ice cubes in the blender if you like.

## Green Smoothie

## Ingredients:

1 c. water
2 c. spinach leaves
2 lettuce leaves
1 tbsp. parsley
1 banana
1 small cucumber
1 t. linseeds

## Prepping Details:

1. Combine all of the smoothie components in a blender.
2. Mix and store in the refrigerator until ready to drink.
3. Blend with some ice cubes with the healthy mixture when serving.

## Kale Smoothie

### Ingredients:

1 c. almond milk
2 c. kale leaves
1 apple
1 banana
Pinch of cinnamon

### Prepping Details:

1. Simply combine all the ingredients and place in the refrigerator for a tasty treat any time.
2. Be sure to have a secure lid on the beverage, so it doesn't pick up the other flavors in the refrigerator.

## Kiwi Smoothie

### Ingredients:

½ c. fresh pineapple
5 kiwis
1 banana
Basil leaves – garnish

### Prepping Details:

1. Prepare the smoothie like all the others – until creamy smooth.
2. Place in the refrigerator in a closed container.
3. Store the basil leaves in a Ziploc bag until ready to serve.

## Mango Smoothie

### Ingredients:

1 carrot
1 orange
2 c. diced mango
For the Garnish: Fresh mint leaves

### Prepping Details:

1.  This tasty beverage is so easy. Just add all of the ingredients in a blender.
2.  Mix well and store in the refrigerator or freezer (in an appropriate container).
3.  Store the mint leaves in a Ziploc bag to keep them fresh.

## Melon Smoothie

### Ingredients:

1 pear
2 slices melon
½ cucumber
2 t. lemon juice
3 freshly snipped mint leaves

### Prepping Details:

1. Another easy summertime or any time beverage. Combine all of the fixings in the blender.
2. Mix well and pour into a closed container or glass.
3. Store in the refrigerator until you are ready to enjoy. Use a separate container for the fresh mint leaves.

## Pineapple Smoothie

## Ingredients:

½ c. of each:
- Strawberry
- Fresh pineapple

1 banana
¼ c. orange juice
Fresh mint
Ice cubes

## Prepping Details:

1. You will love this tropical drink. All you do is add all of the fixings, except the ice cubes and mint.
2. Store the mint separately. Place the smoothie in the refrigerator or freezer – depending on the container used for storage.

# Chapter 4:

## Lunch Specialties

From Avocado to White Beans; you'll find it here!

### Avocado & Tuna Salad Boats

Total Time: 6-7 min.
Servings: 4

### Ingredients:

2 cans (6 oz.) tuna
¼ c. chopped red onion
2 stalks celery – small bits
1 t. balsamic vinegar
2 med. avocados
Pepper & Salt – to taste
4 tbsp. olive oil mayonnaise

### How to Prepare:

1.  Thoroughly drain the tuna. Combine with the rest of the fixings but omit the avocado.
2.  When ready to eat, halve and remove the pit from the avocado and stuff with the prepared stuffing.
3.  Top it off with some tomato slices and red onion. Yummy!

## Prepping Details:

1. Do not cut the avocado until serving time.
2. Divide the tuna salad into 4 small containers.
3. At Mealtime: Slice the avocado in half and add a generous squeeze of lemon juice to both halves to prevent browning.
4. If going to work; cover half of the avocado in the refrigerator. Bring the tuna mixture to work and prepare for lunch.
5. The tuna salad mixture will be great in the refrigerator for 3-4 days. Be sure to store in glass containers for best results.

# Balsamic Beet Salad with Blue Cheese and Walnuts

Total Time: 15 min.
Servings: 4

## Ingredients:

3 c. drained canned beets
¼ c. of each vinegar:
- Red wine
- Balsamic
- Chopped apple

2 tbsp. olive oil
½ t. of each:
- Freshly cracked black pepper
- Kosher salt

8 c. fresh spinach
4 tbsp. chopped walnuts
¼ c. crumbled feta or blue cheese
Fresh mint or parsley – for the garnish

## How to Prepare:

1. Whisk the vinegars, pepper, salt, and oil in one bowl.
2. In another container, blend and toss the remainder of the fixings.
3. Finish up the final details when you are ready to eat. Garnish with some fresh herbs.

## Prepping Details:

1. Prepare the salad and store in a glass or metal container for two days in the refrigerator.
2. Prepare the dressing in another dish and cover with an airtight lid.
3. Also keep the walnuts in a Ziploc bag for freshness.
4. Combine all of the components once you are ready to eat.

## Chicken Bowls

Total Time: 1 hr. – 10 min.
Servings: 5

### Ingredients for the Bowls:

20-25 grape tomatoes
5 handfuls of spinach
½ English cucumber
 1 ¼ c. roasted chickpeas
20 kalamata olives
1 c. red/yellow bell peppers
1 ½ c. grilled chicken
5 oz. feta cheese

### Ingredients for the Tahini Dressing:

1 garlic clove
5 tbsp. tahini
3 tbsp. olive oil
4 t. freshly squeezed lemon juice
5 tbsp. water – as needed
Pepper and Salt - to taste

### Ingredients for the Roasted Chickpeas:

2 tbsp. olive oil
1 can (15 oz.) chickpeas
Salt and Pepper – to your liking

### How to Prepare:

1. Prepare the Fixings: Dice the cucumber and bell peppers. Slice the tomatoes into halves. Thinly slice the chicken, mince the garlic, and crumble the cheese. Drain, rinse, and dry the chickpeas.
2. Prepare the Chickpeas: Set the oven temperature at 350°F. Toss with the oil, salt, and pepper. Arrange in a single layer on a baking tin and bake until crunchy (20-30 min.). Let cool while you make the dressing.

3. Combine all of the fixings for the dressing using a whisk. Add water to reach the desired consistency.
4. Serve if you are ready to eat.

## Prepping Details:

1. Once everything is cooled, arrange the ingredients in 5 separate containers to use when needed.
2. Arrange the spinach in each of the containers, top it off with 4 to 5 tomatoes, cucumber, 1 oz. feta, ¼ c. of the chickpeas, 4 olives, and about 4 ounces of the chicken. Top it off with the peppers and close the lid.
3. Portion the dressing in a separate container.
4. When ready to serve; just add the dressing and enjoy.

## Chilled Artichoke & Zucchini Salad

Total Time: 10 min.
Servings: 4

### Ingredients:

¼ c. extra-virgin olive oil
2 med. breasts of chicken
3 large zucchinis diced – small rounds
2 c. artichoke hearts – from the jar
1 c. kalamata olives
½ t. of each:
- Grated parmesan
- Italian seasoning
- Fresh ground black pepper

### How to Prepare:

1. Dice cooked chicken into 1-inch cubes. Drain the artichoke hearts.
2. Warm up the oil in a skillet and saute the zucchini about 5 minutes. Sprinkle with the salt and pepper. Stir and remove from the burner.
3. Add the rest of the fixings and mix well. Stir and place in a glass bowl. Store in the refrigerator and serve cold.

### Prepping Details:

1. Prepare the salad. You can pre-portion into 4 Tupperware containers for a quick on-the-go meal.
2. You can also leave in the large bowl if you choose. Just be sure it has a tight fighting lid.
3. Store in glass containers for up to 3 days for a fresh salad any time.

## Egg Salad for Lunch

Total Time: 12-15 min.
Servings: 5-6

### Ingredients:

8 large hard-boiled eggs
½ c. of each:
- Chopped cucumber
- Red onion
- Sun-dried tomatoes

¼ c. olives
Splash – lemon juice
½ c. plain Greek yogurt
¼ t. cumin
1 ½ t. oregano
½ t. sea salt
To Taste: Ground black pepper

### How to Prepare:

1. Drain off the excess of oil from the tomatoes. Chop the veggies and eggs.
2. Combine the eggs with the tomatoes, onion, olives, and cucumber.
3. Stir in the spices, lemon juice, and yogurt.
4. Serve and enjoy.

### Prepping Details:

1. Prepare all of the fixings and combine the ingredients as described in step 1 and 2. Place in a closed glass container.
2. Store the spices, yogurt, and lemon in separate containers.
3. When you're ready to eat, just combine all of the fixings and enjoy.
4. It will remain fresh for about one week in the refrigerator.

# Fig & Goat Cheese Salad

Total Time: 6 min.
Servings: 1

## Ingredients:

2 c. mixed salad greens
4 dried figs
1 oz. crumbled fresh goat cheese
1 ½ tbsp. slivered almonds – toasted is best
2 t. olive oil - extra-virgin
½ t. honey
2 t. balsamic vinegar
To Taste:
- Freshly cracked pepper
- Pinch of salt

## How to Prepare:

1. Prepare the salad by combining the greens, figs, cheese, and almonds in a large dish.
2. Mix the vinegar, oil, salt, pepper, and honey together for the dressing.
3. At this point, just enjoy.

## Prepping Details:

1. Prepare one or more salads and place in a closed container.
2. Add the dressing to a separate container.
3. When ready for lunch, just combine and serve.

# Garbanzo Egg Salad with Honey Dijon Vinaigrette

Total Time: 20 min.
Servings: 4

## Ingredients:

1 med. chopped cucumber
½ c. sliced red onion
2 c spinach
6 sliced hard-boiled eggs
1 can (15 oz.) chickpeas
½ c. of each – freshly chopped:
- Mint
- Basil

## Ingredients for the Dressing:

1 large lemon – juice & zest
2 ½ t. Dijon mustard
¼ c. olive oil
½ t. of each:
- Kosher salt
- Garlic powder

2 tbsp. honey
¼ t. freshly cracked black pepper

## How to Prepare:

1. Combine all of the dressings fixings and whisk well.
2. Toss the salad ingredients in another bowl and toss with the dressing (if serving now).

## Prepping Details:

1. Measure out 4 portions into Tupperware-type bowls for packable lunches.
2. Arrange the fixings in layers beginning with the spinach, onion, cucumber, egg, chickpeas and the herbs. Be sure to add the dressing in a separate container.

3. Drizzle with the dressing – only when you are ready to enjoy. Also, be sure to shake the dressing thoroughly before serving.
4. The salads will remain healthy for 3-4 days when stored in the refrigerator without the dressing added.

# Greek Orzo Salad

Total Time: 3 hr. (+)
Servings: 8

## Ingredients:

1 c. uncooked orzo pasta
6 t. canola/olive oil – divided
1 med. finely chopped onion
½ c. minced fresh parsley
1 ½ t. dried oregano
1/3 c. cider or red wine vinegar

## How to Prepare:

1. Prepare and drain the orzo. Add it to a serving dish with two teaspoons of the oil.
2. In another dish mix the parsley, onion, salt, vinegar, sugar, rest of the oil, oregano, and pepper. Pour over the orzo and place in the refrigerator two to 24 hours.
3. Right before serving, stir in the olives, tomatoes, cucumber, and cheese.

## Prepping Details:

1. Prepare all of the ingredients as described. Prepare and drain the orzo and combine with the oil.
2. Mix the rest of the fixings and store in the refrigerator for a minimum of 2 hours or as much as 24 hours.
3. Prepare the salads in individual containers using the desired serving amounts and store in the refrigerator.
4. You can measure out the rest of the fixings and store in separate containers to save some time later, or you can do it all when serving.

## Greek Salad In A Jar

Total Time: 5 min.
Servings: 4

## Ingredients:

5 c. torn mixed salad greens
1 large chopped cucumber
2 sliced Roma tomatoes
½ c. sliced black olives
¼ c sliced red onion
1 can (15 oz.) chickpeas
1 tbsp. lemon juice
3 tbsp. olive oil
1/8 t. pepper
¼ t. salt
½ c. crumbled feta cheese
Also Needed: 4 medium-sized Mason jars

## How to Prepare:

1. Whisk the oil, lemon, pepper, and salt in a small mixing container.
2. Rinse and drain the chickpeas. Add them to each of the jars.
3. Pour the mixture (step 1) over the beans.
4. Next add the cucumber, olives, onions, and tomatoes. Add the greens along with the feta cheese. Enjoy!

## Prepping Details:

1. Store the prepared jars in the refrigerator for up to 4 days.
2. Before Serving: Shake well and toss. Smile!

# Greek Tacos

Total Time: 8 min.
Servings: 4

## Ingredients:

4 c. chopped Romaine lettuce
2 med. shredded chicken breasts
1 c. yellow or red cherry tomatoes – halved
¾ c. diced cucumbers
2 tbsp. chopped fresh mint
½ c. sliced black olives
1 c. crumbled feta cheese
¼ c. of each:
- Olive oil
- Balsamic vinegar

¼ t. black pepper
½ t. kosher salt
1/3 cucumber dill Greek yogurt dip
8 low carb mini wraps or 8 small whole grain tortillas

## How to Prepare:

1. Combine the shredded chicken with the olives, cucumber, tomatoes, and mint. Sprinkle with the oil, vinegar, pepper, and salt. Toss.
2. Prepare the Tacos: Divide the mixture into eighths. Scoop onto the wrap/tortilla and add the lettuce. Top it off with the feta and a dollop of the yogurt dip.

## Prepping Details:

1. Prepare the taco mixture and store in a glass container in the refrigerator. It will be good for up to 3 days.
2. Store the tomatoes and lettuce in separate Ziploc bags.
3. You can prepare the tacos right before lunch or in the morning before it's time to leave for work.
4. Roll each one into waxed paper and refrigerate until ready to eat. Keep in an airtight container.

# Lebanese Tabbouleh

Total Time: 40-45 minutes
Servings: 4

## Ingredients:

½ c. bulgur wheat
1 c. firm tomatoes
1 med. cucumber
¼ c. fresh mint
2 c. Italian parsley – loosely packed
1/3 c. green onion
¼ c. of each:
- Fresh lemon juice
- Extra-virgin olive oil

Optional: Baby spinach
To Taste: Salt & Pepper

## How to Prepare:

1. Do the Prep: Finely chop the tomatoes and dice the cucumbers. Remove the stems from the parsley and chop it along with the mint and onion.
2. Place the wheat in a small bowl and cover with water to soak (5-6 min.). Drain the water and place in a towel to remove the excess liquids.
3. Combine all of the fixings and give it a shake of pepper and salt.
4. Chill for 30 minutes before serving.

## Prepping Details:

1. Reserve the oil and lemon juice until you're ready to prepare your meal.
2. You can store for up to 3 days without the additions for up to 3 days.
3. Combine and enjoy.

## Quinoa Spinach Salad in a Mason Jar

Total Time: 20-25 min.
Servings: 4

## Ingredients:

3 c. greens – your choice – ex. arugula or baby spinach
1 can (15 oz.) chickpeas
2 minced cloves of garlic
¼ c. of each:
- Sliced black olives
- Roasted red peppers – minced from a jar

1 ½ c. dry quinoa
1/3 c. olive oil
1 tbsp. red wine vinegar
½ t. of each – dried & crushed:
- Thyme
- Basil
- Salt
- Freshly cracked pepper

Optional:
- Cherry tomatoes
- Fresh basil

Also Needed: 4 Mason jars

## How to Prepare:

1. Cook the quinoa according to the package instructions. Let it cool before using
2. Combine the vinegar, salt, pepper, thyme, basil, and oil in a small mixing container.
3. Prepare the Jars: Add the chickpeas, olives, and red peppers. Measure out the dressing and pour over the fixings in each of the jars. For the next layer, add quinoa and lastly top it off with the greens.
4. Seal the jar and place in the refrigerator.
5. Serve with tomatoes if you like it that way.

## Prepping Details:

1. Leave the prepared jars in the refrigerator until you are ready to use.
2. Shake well before enjoying.
3. You can keep this tasty luncheon snack for 3-4 days in the refrigerator.

# Roasted Carrot Ginger Bisque

Total Time: 1 hr. – 14 min.
Servings: 6-8

## Ingredients:

3 lb. carrots
2 tbsp. olive oil
4 minced garlic cloves
2-inch piece fresh ginger root
5 c. vegetable stock
2 t. freshly chopped cilantro
1 t. allspice
1 c. milk
½ c. Greek yogurt
As Desired: Freshly cracked black pepper & Kosher salt

## How to Prepare:

1. Warm up the oven to 425°F.
2. Peel the carrots and cover well with the oil. Shake on the spices, pepper, and salt.
3. Roast the carrots for 40-50 minutes until they're caramelized. (Flip after about 25 minutes.) Remove and cool.
4. Chop into cubes and add to a food processor. Pour in the broth, garlic, and ginger. Pulse until chunks are removed.
5. Pour into a cooking pot. Toss in the cilantro and allspice. Cook slowly for about 10 minutes (med. heat).
6. Lower the heat and add the milk and yogurt.
7. Remove from the pot and serve with the fresh parsley the way you like it.

## Prepping Details:

1. Prepare the bisque and store in a metal or glass container for up to 4 days.
2. Enjoy anytime and warm up over low heat on the stovetop for the best results.

## Turkey Taco Lunch Bowls

Total Time: 1 hr. – 10 min.
Servings: 4

### Ingredients:

### Turkey:

2 tbsp. taco seasoning – your choice
¾ lb. lean ground turkey

### Rice:

¾ c. uncooked brown rice
Zest 1 lime
1/8 t. salt

### Salsa:

1 minced jalapeno
1 pint - quartered cherry tomatoes
¼ c. minced red onion
1 minced jalapeno
½ lime – juiced
1/8 t. salt

### Other Fixings:

1 can (12 oz.) kernel corn – drained
¼ c. shredded mozzarella or cheddar cheese

### How to Prepare:

1. Cook the rice according to the package instructions. Mix in the salt and lime zest to the water.
2. Cook the ground turkey (med. heat) along with the taco seasoning. Prepare about 10 minutes.

## Prepping Details:

1. Prep for 4 Servings: Use (1) 4-compartment tray for each serving and ¼ portion of the prepared rice (approx. ½ cup), ½ cup of the corn, ½ cup of the taco meat, and ¼ portion of the salsa (approx. ½ cup).
2. You may also add each of the ingredients to separate bowls if you choose. Then, you would add each of the fixings into the waiting serving dishes.
3. Make as many variations as you desire.

## White Bean Soup

Total Time: 7-10 min.
Servings: 4

### Ingredients:

2 t. extra-virgin olive oil
1 large of each – sliced into rounds:
- Carrot
- Leek

2 c. shredded chicken
½ t. of each:
- Italian seasoning
- Sage

Pepper and Salt
1 can (15 oz.) cannellini beans
28 oz. chicken broth
2 c. water

### How to Prepare:

1. Warm up the oil in a large stewpot to prepare the carrots and leeks. Saute about 4 minutes.
2. Sprinkle with the salt, pepper, and seasonings. Continue cooking about 1 more minute. Stir in the rest of the fixings.
3. Cook until it reaches the desired consistency and flavor.
4. Note: It should take one whole chicken to get the 2 cups of chicken.

### Prepping Details:

1. Prepare the entire batch of soup. Store it in the refrigerator in one bowl or in individual bowls. Make sure the tops are secure.
2. When it's time to eat, just pour into a pan on the stovetop, and. Serve the healthy soup and relax.

# White Bean & Tuna Lettuce Wraps

Total Time: 12 min.
Servings: 4

## Ingredients:

1 can drained (12 oz.) tuna
8 Bibb lettuce leaves
¼ c. chopped red onion
1 can (15 oz.) drained & rinsed cannellini beans
½ c. corn
2 tbsp of each:
- Olive oil
- Balsamic vinegar

1/8 t. of each: Salt & Pepper
1 tbsp. minced fresh basil
1 med. ripe avocado – diced

## How to Prepare:

1. Rinse and drain the beans. Also, rinse the lettuce and dry with a spinner or paper towels.
2. Combine the rest of the fixings.
3. Portion the tuna into 4 Tupperware containers.
4. Before Serving: Spoon 1/8 of the mixture into the leaves of lettuce. Tuck in the edges like a regular wrap.

## Prepping Details:

1. Prepare the tuna and add it to the containers. It is safe in the refrigerator for 3 days. Store the leaves of lettuce in a separate bag or dish.
2. Prepare when you are ready to serve.

# Chapter 5:

## Dinner Favorites

Enjoy dinner the way all the Mediterranean folks do!

### Oven-Roasted Garlic Chicken Thighs

Total Time: 1 hr. - 18 min.
Servings: 6-8

### Ingredients:

1 ½ lb. potatoes
8 chicken thighs
1 tbsp. EVOO
Pepper and Salt – to taste
6 garlic cloves
1 jar (10 oz.) roasted red peppers
1/3 c. capers/green olives
2 c. cherry tomatoes
1 t. dried Italian seasoning
1 tbsp. fresh basil

### How to Prepare:

1.  Do the Prep: Slice the tomatoes into halves and dice the potatoes. Peel and dice the garlic cloves. Then drain the red peppers and chop them into bits.
2.  Warm the oven to 400°F.
3.  Sprinkle the chicken with the pepper and salt. Sear in the hot olive oil (med.-high) in a cast iron skillet.

4. Transfer to the oven and bake for 45 minutes (165°F internal temp.)

## Prepping Details:

1. Wrap the chicken in foil and store for up to three days in the refrigerator.
2. Remove from the foil. Warm up in the microwave with 1 teaspoon of water to prevent dryness while heating.

## Pork Loin & Orzo

Total Time: 20-23 min.
Servings: 4

### Ingredients:

1 lb. pork tenderloin
2 tbsp. olive oil
1 t. of each:
- Kosher salt
- Coarse ground pepper

1 c. uncooked orzo pasta
2 c. spinach
Water
1 c. halved cherry tomatoes
¾ c. feta cheese

### How to Prepare:

1. Make a rub with the salt and pepper. Coat the loin with the rub and dice into 1-inch cubes.
2. Prepare a cast iron skillet using the medium heat setting to warm up the oil. Cook the pork for about 8 minutes.
3. Follow the package instructions for the orzo and toss in a pinch or so of salt into the water. Fold in the tomatoes and spinach. Add the cooked pork and top with the feta.

### Prepping Details:

1. Prepare the meal ahead of time. Store - ready-to-go - in a glass container for up to 3 days. You could also divide it up and take some for a quick lunch at work.
2. Warm it up over the stovetop or in the microwave. It's also good cold!

# Slow-Cooked Pork Tenderloin & Quinoa Salad

Total Time: 3 hr. – 15 min.
Servings: 6

## Ingredients:

1 ½ lb. pork tenderloin
¼ c. olive oil
¼ t. black pepper
½ t. kosher salt
4 minced cloves of garlic
1 c. of each:
- Chicken broth
- Quinoa

2 tbsp. apple cider vinegar
½ c. of each:
- Freshly minced parsley
- Dried cranberries

Toasted & sliced almonds

## How to Prepare:

1. Empty the broth into the slow cooker.
2. Rub the pork with the pepper, salt, and half of the minced garlic. Arrange in the cooker. Prepare on low for 2 hours (160°F – internal temp.). Transfer to a cutting board.
3. Dump the juices from the cooker into a measuring cup. Pour back 1 cup of the liquids and add the quinoa. Cook for 15 minutes or until fluffy.
4. Add the cranberries and almonds. Mix well.
5. In another mixing bowl, whisk the vinegar, ½ t. salt, ¼ t. pepper, oil, garlic, and parsley. Mix the vinaigrette well.
6. Slice the tenderloin and serve with the quinoa and a drizzle of vinaigrette.

## Prepping Details:

1. Prepare the meal ahead of time and just reheat.
2. Pour the vinaigrette into a separate container and add when dinner is ready.

3. Store the pork and quinoa separately up to 3 days in the refrigerator. It is best to use glass containers or airtight Ziploc bags.
4. Microwave or reheat in the slow cooker.

# Spiced Salmon & Vegetable Quinoa

Total Time: 40 min.
Servings: 4-5

## Ingredients:

2 c. water
1 c. uncooked quinoa
½ t. kosher salt
1 c. cherry tomatoes
¾ c. English cucumbers
¼ c. red onion
4 basil leaves
1 lemon – zested

## Salmon Ingredients:

¼ t. black pepper
½ t. of each:
- Paprika
- Kosher salt

1 t. cumin
4 (5 oz.) salmon fillets (total 20 oz.)
8 lemon wedges
¼ c. freshly chopped parsley

## How to Prepare:

1. Prep the Veggies: Remove the seeds from the cucumbers and dice with the onion. Slice the tomatoes into halves. Chop the basil leaves.
2. Warm up the oven to broil.
3. Lightly grease a glass dish or sheet pan with some spray or olive oil.
4. Mix the water, quinoa, and salt in a pot. Once it boils, put a lid on, and cook slowly for approximately 20 minutes (or per package instructions).
5. Turn off the heat and cool five minutes covered before eating. To mix; combine the cucumbers, onions, tomatoes, lemon zest, and basil.

6. Prepare the Salmon: Mix the paprika, cumin, salt, and pepper. Coat the fillets with about ½ teaspoon of the mixture. Add lemon on the edge of the pan and broil on high using the lower third of the oven for 8-10 minutes.

7. Sprinkle the salmon with some parsley, a lemon wedge, and a side of quinoa.

## Prepping Details:

1. Prepare the salmon, quinoa, and veggies as shown above but place them into separate containers if you want to have as a meal later. Combine then.

2. You can also prep the fixings for each serving into the number of containers (4 or 5) but don't add the lemon wedge and parsley to the dishes until ready to serve.

## Stuffed Peppers in The Slow Cooker

Total Time: 6 hr. – 45 min.
Servings: 6

## Ingredients:

6 bell peppers
2 t. extra-virgin olive oil
1 onion
½ lb. ground beef
1 c. garbanzo beans
1 t. of each:
- Italian seasoning
- Kosher salt

½ t. garlic powder
¼ t. of each:
- Cayenne pepper
- Freshly cracked black pepper

½ c chopped parsley
2 c. brown rice
1 can (15 oz.) tomato sauce

## How to Prepare:

1. Prep the Fixings: Cook the rice according to package instructions. Remove the tops from the peppers and scoop out the seeds. Chop the onion and parsley.
2. Heat up a skillet using the medium heat setting and add the oil. Saute the onions 3-5 minutes. Toss in the beef and cook until it's no longer pink.
3. Empty into a mixing container and combine the rest of the fixings except for the peppers and sauce.
4. Mix well and portion into the six peppers.
5. Arrange in the slow cooker and add the sauce. Prepare for 6 hours.
6. *Note:* Make this a special one since it has red meat and is not as popular on the Mediterranean diet plan.

## Prepping Details:

1. Store in the refrigerator for up to 3 days. Warm up in the microwave.
2. You can also prep the night before and let it cook all day and be ready for dinner.
3. Freeze any unused peppers for later.

# Turkey Lentil Meatballs with Tzatziki Dipping Sauce

Total Time: 30-35 min.
Servings: 4

## Ingredients:

1 c. cooked brown lentils
1 lb. lean ground turkey
½ c. panko breadcrumbs
2 eggs
2 minced garlic cloves
2 tbsp. of each:
- Capers
- Finely minced red onion

¼ c. feta cheese
1 tbsp. Greek seasoning
1 t. kosher salt
½ t. freshly cracked black pepper
1 c. Tzatziki dipping sauce

## How to Prepare:

1. Preheat the oven to 375°F.
2. Pulse the lentils in a blender and combine all of the fixings except the tzatziki sauce. Mix in a large bowl using your hands.
3. Make about 20 meatballs (5 per serving). Prepare on a greased baking pan for 20 minutes.
4. Enjoy with the Tzatziki dipping sauce and a bit of fresh lemon over its top.

## Prepping Details:

1. Store the meatballs up to 3 days in the refrigerator or place them in the freezer.
2. When it is time to eat, just place them in a glass microwavable dish with 1 tablespoon of water.
3. Prepare each serving with ¼ cup of the sauce. Give it a sprinkle of fresh lemon and serve.

## Tuscan Artichoke Salad

Total Time: 15-20 min.
Servings: 4

## Ingredients:

3 minced cloves of garlic
1 small sliced red onion
1 pkg. (18 oz.) frozen artichokes
1 can (28 oz.) crushed tomatoes
1 tbsp. extra-virgin olive oil
½ c. white wine
1 tbsp. freshly squeezed lemon juice
1/3 c. freshly grated parmesan
Pepper and Salt to taste
For the Garnish: Sundried tomatoes

## How to Prepare:

1. Warm up the olive oil in a frying pan and add the onion. Saute until it begins softening and add the garlic. Stir frequently.
2. Stir in the wine and continue cooking until the liquid is reduced to about ½ of its original volume.
3. Fold in the artichokes, tomatoes, pepper, salt, and lemon juice.
4. Serve with a topping of sun-dried tomatoes and parmesan.

## Prepping Details:

1. Prepare ahead of time and let it cool.
2. Either add it into four containers or in one glass bowl. It is best to store the sundried tomatoes and parmesan in separate containers.
3. Store the salad in the refrigerator up to 4 days. Warm up in the microwave for a tasty lunch or dinner treat.

# Tuscan Style Tuna Salad

Total Time: 6 min.
Servings: 4

## Ingredients:

1 can (15 oz.) small white beans – such as great northern/cannellini
2 cans (6 oz. ea.) drained – chunk light tuna
10 cherry tomatoes
4 scallions
¼ t. salt
2 tbsp. lemon juice
Pepper to taste

## How to Prepare:

1. Prep the Salad: Quarter the tomatoes. Trim the scallions and slice. Drain the beans and juice a lemon for the best results. Drain the tuna.
2. Combine all of the ingredients in a covered container.
3. Stir gently and refrigerate until ready to eat.

## Prepping Details:

1. Prepare the salad fixings and store in a glass covered container, or you can also arrange the salads in four individual serving trays. Be sure to close the lids securely to keep everything fresh.
2. Measure out and store the veggies and lemons separately until ready to use. It is best to slice the lemon when you are ready to eat unless you want the salad on-the-go.

## Vegetable Thin Crust Pizza

Total Time: 45-50 minutes
Servings: 4

## Ingredients for the Crust:

½ c. hot water
1 ¼ c. whole wheat flour
½ t. yeast
1 pinch of salt
2 t. honey

## Ingredients for the Toppings:

Olive oil
½ c. of each:
- Tomato sauce
- Greek yogurt

½ t. garlic powder
¼ t. oregano
¼ c. chopped black olives
1 ½ c. shredded mozzarella
½ c. chopped green onions
1 c. chopped of each:
- Spinach
- Cremini mushrooms – or slice

1 small tomato – in rounds

## How to Prepare:

1. Preheat the oven to 425°F.
2. Combine the honey and yeast with the warm water – not hot. Allow the yeast to foam and activate in a mixing bowl.
3. Stir in the flour and drizzle with the oil. Mix and shape into a ball.
4. Let the dough rise (10-15 min.). Punch it down and spread it out thinly over a pizza stone or baking sheet. Bake for 5 minutes.
5. Mix the tomato sauce, garlic powder, oregano, salt, pepper, and yogurt.

6. Spread out over the crust and add the cheese, then the toppings.

7. Bake until the cheese is melted and the crust is crisp (10-15 min.).

## Prepping Details:

1. Prepare the pizza crust and bake for 5 minutes. The crust is good in the refrigerator for up to 4 days. You can also freeze for later.

2. When you're ready for pizza, remove the crust and pour on the sauce. Add whatever you choose for the toppings.

3. Prep the veggies in advance and alternate the toppings for a unique pizza every time.

4. Bake at 425°F for 10-15 minutes and enjoy.

## Sides

## Baked Zucchini Sticks

Total Time: 35 min.
Servings: 8

## Ingredients:

4 med. zucchini
½ c. of each:
- Kalamata olives
- Tomatoes

3 large cloves of garlic
1 tbsp. dried oregano
¼ t. black pepper
¼ c. of each:
- Feta cheese
- Parsley

## How to Prepare:

1. Preheat the oven to 350°F.
2. Slice the zucchini lengthwise and into halves. Remove the middle and discard the flesh. Finely chop the veggies and mince the cloves.
3. Use a medium dish and add the tomatoes, peppers, garlic, black pepper, and oregano.
4. Spread the mixture into the zucchini and arrange on a baking dish. Bake 15 minutes and top with the feta. Bake another three minutes until the cheese has browned.
5. Serve hot or cold with a sprinkle of parsley.

## Prepping Details:

1. Prepare the zucchini but don't add the feta until you are ready to eat.
2. If you choose, you can also add the feta and brown it until done. Put it in some aluminum foil or other container and place in the refrigerator until ready to eat.

3. Add the parsley when serving.

## Lentil & Garlic Bowls

Total Time: 40-45 min.
Servings: 4-6

## Ingredients:

6 minced garlic cloves
2 diced onions
1 tbsp. olive oil
2 c. rinsed dried lentils
½ t. of each:
- Paprika
- Ground ginger
3 c. vegetable broth
1 t. kosher salt
¼ t. pepper
¾ c. Greek yogurt
3 tbsp. tomato paste
¼ c. lemon juice

## How to Prepare:

1. In a soup pot; heat the oil and saute the onions for about 4-5 minutes using the medium heat setting. When the edges start to brown, add the garlic and saute about 2 more minutes.
2. Pour in the broth and lentils. Once boiling, lower the heat and simmer about 30 minutes or until tender.
3. Stir in the rest of the fixings and serve.

## Prepping Details:

1. Prepare the meal and store in a glass container in the refrigerator. It's delicious for up to 3 days.
2. Pop it into the microwave to heat or eat it right out of the refrigerator.

## Mediterranean Vegetables

Total Time: 11 min.
Servings: 4-5

### Ingredients:

2 med. zucchini
1 med. yellow onion
1 small red bell pepper
2 tbsp. (+) 2 t. extra-virgin olive oil – divided
2 t. of each:
- Balsamic vinegar
- Greek seasonings

¼ t. of each:
- Garlic salt
- Sugar

### How to Prepare:

1. Slice the zucchinis into eights; lengthwise, then halved – about 3-inches long.
2. Pour two tablespoons of the oil in a skillet to warm. Add the onion, zucchini, and peppers. Saute 6 minutes.
3. Combine the rest of the oil and ingredients in a small dish.
4. Add the seasonings to the veggies and serve.

### Prepping Details:

1. Prepare and cook the zucchini. Arrange in individual containers to be used with one of your special entrees.
2. Don't add the seasonings until it's mealtime.

## Pan-Seared Eggplant Medallions with Balsamic Reduction

Total Time: 35 min.
Servings: 6

### Ingredients:

2 large/3 med. eggplants
1 c. balsamic vinegar
2 tbsp. honey
¼ t. black pepper
½ t. kosher salt
2 tbsp. olive oil
4 eggs
2 tbsp. fresh mint

### How to Prepare:

1.  Slice the eggplants into ½-inch rounds and chop the mint. Set aside.
2.  Warm up the vinegar and stir in the honey using a small saucepan. Whisk until it boils. Lower the heat and simmer about 20 minutes. The vinegar will begin thickening.
3.  Warm up the oil in a cast-iron skillet and sear the eggplant 3-4 minutes per side. Sprinkle with the pepper and salt.
4.  In another frying pan, prepare the eggs the way you like them.
5.  Portion out each serving and add a fried egg to the top. Give it a drizzle of the balsamic reduction and garnish with some freshly chopped mint.

### Prepping Details:

1.  Prepare the balsamic sauce in advance. Slice the eggplant and store in a Ziploc bag or storage container.
2.  When it's dinner time, fry the eggplant and eggs.
3.  Serve and enjoy!

## Roasted Zucchini with Yogurt & Dill

Total Time: 40 min.
Servings: 4

## Ingredients:

1 lb. 1-inch cubes
½ sweet Vidalia onion
2 tbsp. extra-virgin olive oil
4 minced garlic cloves
¼ t. black pepper
½ t. kosher salt
¼ c. slivered almonds
Pepper & Kosher salt – to taste
2/3 c. Greek yogurt
1 ½ tbsp. fresh dill

## How to Prepare:

1. Preheat the oven to 400°F.
2. Peel and chop the zucchini into cubes and add to a mixing container with the onion, garlic, salt, and pepper.
3. Layer the zucchini on a baking tin. Bake for 25-30 minutes.
4. Let it slightly cool. Toss the veggies into the yogurt and top with the fresh dill and almonds.
5. Serve and enjoy.

## Prepping Details:

1. Prepare all of the veggies. Wait to roast them. Add to a plastic Ziploc bag.
2. When you are ready to eat, roast and add the favorite toppings.

# Chapter 6:

## Desserts

### Almond & Honey Peaches

Total Time: 20 min.
Servings: 4-5

**Ingredients:**

1 can peaches
2 tbsp. honey
¼ t. cardamom
½ c. low-fat ricotta cheese
¼ c. almonds

**How to Prepare:**

1.  Warm up the oven to 400°F.
2.  Rinse the peaches and cut into halves. Arrange on a cookie tin.
3.  Combine the cheese with the cardamom and honey. Spoon the fixings into the halves. Bake for 15 minutes.
4.  Using a food processor, coarsely ground the almonds and toast over medium heat in a skillet.
5.  Sprinkle the nuts over the peaches and enjoy.

**Prepping Details:**

1.  Prepare the peaches and bake for 15 minutes. Store in a glass bowl or in individual containers for a quick on-the-go treat.

2. Process the almonds and toast but don't add it to the peaches. Store in a Ziploc bag or other container.
3. When ready to eat, just sprinkle the nuts over the peaches.

## Baked Apple – Mediterranean Style

Total Time: 50 min.
Servings: 4

### Ingredients:

4 cooking apples
4 tbsp. honey
¼ t. of each:
- Nutmeg
- Allspice

½ t. ground cinnamon
½ c. chopped of each:
- Almonds/walnuts
- Golden raisins

½ lemon - juice & zest

### How to Prepare:

1. Warm up the oven to 350°F.
2. Core the apples and arrange them in a baking pan.
3. Combine the rest of the fixings and fill the cores. Use the rest scooped on the top.
4. Pour ½-inch of water into the baking dish. Add the apples and arrange on the middle shelf of the oven. Bake 40-45 minutes – or to your liking.
5. Place the apples on serving plates. Pour the juices from the baking dish over them and enjoy.

### Prepping Details:

1. Bake the apples as shown above.
2. Place each of the apples into a piece of foil. Warm up later in the oven for best results.
3. Store the juices in individual dishes or a closed container.

# Fruit Salad with Honey Mint Sauce

Total Time: 5-8 min.
Servings: 4-5

## Ingredients:

½ apple
¼ banana
¼ c. of each:
- Blueberries
- Raspberries
- Strawberries

½ plum
½ peach
1 tbsp. mint
1 mint-flavored tea bag
¼ tbsp. lemon juice
½ tbsp. honey
1/3 c. water

## How to Prepare:

1. Peel and cube the apple. Remove the pits from the plum and peach. Chop the mint and remove the banana peeling.
2. Pour the water into a small saucepan. Once it boils, add the tea bag, juice, and honey. Simmer for a minute or two until it's like you like it. Set aside to cool.
3. Mix the fruit in a container and pour the mixture into the bowl. Mix and place in the refrigerator to chill.
4. Serve with a sprinkle of fresh mint.

## Prepping Details:

1. Prepare the sauce (as shown above) and store in a jar with a lid or divide into separate containers. Also, divide the fruit into the desired containers.
2. Stash the fresh mint in a Ziploc bag.
3. When you are in a hurry grab a container of each and enjoy.

## Greek Yogurt Parfait

Total Time: 5 minutes
Servings: 4

### Ingredients:

¼ c. chopped dried dates
¾ c. whole grain unsweetened granola
2 c. unsweetened Greek yogurt
4 t. honey
1/8 c. slivered toasted almonds

### How to Prepare:

1. Pour ¼ cup of the yogurt into the bottom of a serving glass or jar. Add some granola, a layer of yogurt, granola, dates, almonds, and a drizzle of 1 t. of honey.
2. Do this in all four jars and enjoy or store.

### Prepping Details:

1. Prep this one by having all of the fixings premeasured.
2. All you will need to do is combine when it is time to run.

# Chapter 7:
## 30-Day Meal Plan

You will enjoy the freedom you will have once you have decided how to prep your meals ahead of time. The healthy ways the Mediterranean style provide will surely give you the nutrition you need daily. This plan is not written in stone but is a simple guideline using your new 51 recipes to prepare a 1-month plan.

Let's get started:

**Day 1:**
**Breakfast:** Breakfast Quinoa with Dates & Apricots
**Lunch:** Chicken Bowls
**Dinner:** Vegetable Thin Crust Pizza

**Day 2:**
**Breakfast:** Avocado Smoothie
**Lunch:** Balsamic Beet Salad with Blue Cheese & Walnuts
**Dinner:** Oven-Roasted Garlic Chicken Thighs
**Side:** Baked Zucchini Sticks

**Day 3:**
**Breakfast:** Cranberry Breakfast Muffins
**Lunch:** Avocado & Tuna Salad Boats
**Dinner:** Stuffed Peppers in The Slow Cooker
**Dessert:** Almond & Honey Peaches

**Day 4:**
**Breakfast:** Tuscan Veggie Frittata
**Lunch:** Chilled Artichoke & Zucchini Salad

**Dinner:** Pork Loin & Orzo
**Side:** Lentil & Garlic Bowls

**Day 5:**
**Breakfast:** Beetroot Smoothie
**Lunch:** Egg Salad
**Dinner:** Stuffed Peppers in The Slow Cooker
**Dessert:** Baked Apple – Mediterranean Style

**Day 6:**
**Breakfast:** Green Smoothie
**Lunch:** Fig & Goat Cheese Salad
**Dinner:** Slow-Cooked Pork Tenderloin & Quinoa Salad

**Day 7:**
**Breakfast:** Strawberry Mango Smoothie with Greek Yogurt
**Lunch:** Greek Orzo Salad
**Dinner:** Spiced Salmon & Vegetable Quinoa

**Day 8:**
**Breakfast:** Coconut Ginger Overnight Oats
**Lunch:** Garbanzo Egg Salad with Honey Dijon Vinaigrette
**Dinner:** Turkey Lentil Meatballs with Tzatziki Dipping Sauce
**Side:** Mediterranean Vegetables

**Day 9:**
**Breakfast:** Breakfast Quinoa with Dates & Apricots
**Lunch:** Greek Salad in A Jar
**Dinner:** Vegetable Thin Crust Pizza
**Dessert:** Fruit Salad with Honey Mint Sauce

**Day 10:**
**Breakfast:** Kiwi Smoothie
**Lunch:** Greek Tacos
**Dinner:** Tuscan Style Tuna Salad
**Dessert:** Greek Yogurt Parfait

**Day 11:**
**Breakfast:** Honey Walnut Overnight Oats
**Lunch:** Lebanese Tabbouleh
**Dinner:** Tuscan Artichoke Salad
**Dessert:** Almond & Honey Peaches

**Day 12:**
**Breakfast:** Pineapple Smoothie
**Lunch:** Quinoa Spinach Salad in a Mason Jar
**Dinner:** Slow-Cooked Pork Tenderloin & Quinoa Salad
**Dessert:** Baked Apple – Mediterranean Style

**Day 13:**
**Breakfast:** Kale Smoothie
**Lunch:** Roasted Carrot Ginger Bisque
**Dinner:** Spiced Salmon & Vegetable Quinoa

**Day 14:**
**Breakfast:** Polenta with Banana
**Lunch:** Turkey Taco Lunch Bowls
**Dinner:** Stuffed Peppers in The Slow Cooker
**Dessert:** Fruit Salad with Honey Mint Sauce

**Day 15:**
**Breakfast:** Breakfast Blueberries & Slow Cooked Quinoa
**Lunch:** White Bean Soup
**Dinner:** Vegetable Thin Crust Pizza
**Dessert:** Greek Yogurt Parfait

**Day 16:**
**Breakfast:** Mango Smoothie
**Lunch:** Avocado & Tuna Salad Boats
**Dinner:** Pork Loin & Orzo
**Side:** Pan-Seared Eggplant Medallions with Balsamic Reduction

**Day 17:**
**Breakfast:** Cranberry Breakfast Muffins
**Lunch:** White Bean & Tuna Lettuce Wraps
**Dinner:** Turkey Lentil Meatballs with Tzatziki Dipping Sauce
**Side:** Roasted Zucchini with Yogurt & Dill

**Day 18:**
**Breakfast:** Tofu Breakfast Scramble
**Lunch:** Chicken Bowls
**Dinner:** Stuffed Peppers in The Slow Cooker
**Dessert:** Almond & Honey Peaches

**Day 19:**
**Breakfast:** Tuscan Veggie Frittata
**Lunch:** Balsamic Beet Salad with Blue Cheese & Walnuts
**Dinner:** Slow-Cooked Pork Tenderloin & Quinoa Salad
**Dessert:** Baked Apple – Mediterranean Style

**Day 20:**
**Breakfast:** Honey Walnut Overnight Oats
**Lunch:** Chilled Artichoke & Zucchini Salad
**Dinner:** Vegetable Thin Crust Pizza

**Day 21:**
**Breakfast:** Polenta with Banana
**Lunch:** Garbanzo Egg Salad with Honey Dijon Vinaigrette
**Dinner:** Oven-Roasted Garlic Chicken Thighs
**Side:** Baked Zucchini Sticks

**Day 22:**
**Breakfast:** Mango Smoothie
**Lunch:** Chilled Artichoke and Zucchini Salad
**Dinner:** Vegetable Thin Crust Pizza

**Day 23:**
**Breakfast:** Pineapple Smoothie
**Lunch:** Greek Salad in A Jar
**Dinner:** Turkey Lentil Meatballs with Tzatziki Dipping Sauce
**Dessert:** Fruit Salad with Honey Mint Sauce

**Day 24:**
**Breakfast:** Breakfast Blueberries & Slow Cooked Quinoa
**Lunch:** White Bean Soup
**Dinner:** Spiced Salmon & Vegetable Quinoa
**Side:** Lentil & Garlic Bowls

**Day 25:**
**Breakfast:** Melon Smoothie
**Lunch:** Turkey Taco Lunch Bowls
**Dinner:** Tuscan Style Tuna Salad

**Day 26:**
**Breakfast:** Kiwi Smoothie
**Lunch:** Egg Salad
**Dinner:** Slow-Cooked Pork Tenderloin & Quinoa Salad

**Day 27:**
**Breakfast:** Cranberry Breakfast Muffins
**Lunch:** Quinoa Spinach Salad in a Mason Jar
**Dinner:** Vegetable Thin Crust Pizza
**Dessert:** Greek Yogurt Parfait

**Day 28:**
**Breakfast:** Tuscan Veggie Frittata
**Lunch:** Chicken Bowls
**Dinner:** Slow-Cooked Pork Tenderloin & Quinoa Salad

**Day 29:**
**Breakfast:** Breakfast Quinoa with Dates & Apricots
**Lunch:** Balsamic Beet Salad with Blue Cheese & Walnuts
**Dinner:** Spiced Salmon & Vegetable Quinoa
**Dessert:** Almond & Honey Peaches

**Day 30:**
**Breakfast:** Melon Smoothie
**Lunch:** White Bean & Tuna Lettuce Wraps
**Dinner:** Pork Loin & Orzo
**Side:** Mediterranean Vegetables

You now have the roadmap to know how to make the plan work. You know you can do it but here are just a few more ways for you to get tuned into using the Mediterranean way of eating. The Mediterranean Diet will allow you the freedom to lose a few extra pounds and not be hungry. This goal is a main element in changing your lifestyle.

## Change Your Eating Habits

*Consider These Changes:*

## Consideration #1:
**Do you like to experiment with new recipes?**

If so, you are like many of the people who have a standard set of recipes. With the Mediterranean diet, you have so many healthy and tasty recipes to test. Your experiment should be loaded with fun. Try to add a new recipe to your list every week. Besides if you have leftovers, most of the meals can be used as a lunchtime meal the following day.

## Consideration #2:
### Do you scoop up second servings on a regular basis?

This behavior can become a bad habit, especially if you are dining with friends and don't want to hurt the host or hostess' feelings. It is acceptable to refuse the additional portions, just let him, or her know you are on a special Mediterranean diet. Maybe he or she will use one of the meals that are healthier on your next visit.

## Consideration #3: Mood Eating:
### Are you increasing your large portions to extra-large portions when you have a meal out or at home?

Make a huge effort toward portion control and don't go by the old standard placed by Grandma. Leave some of the food on the plate. You can always play a mind trick and use a smaller dish. That is a secret that will encourage you to use smaller portions.

## Consideration #3: The Cravings:
### What do you hunger for when you crave a snack?

If it is a piece of cake or a piece of chocolate, change it to a piece of fruit. You will discover many ways to convert sweets to a healthy substitute.

## Consideration #4:
### Are you 'physically' hungry?

Your appetite is a very powerful factor which provides the desire to eat which is why it is sometimes so difficult to lose weight. It is also true that each person has a different threshold of hunger. The feeling is not always a physical need for food.

## Consideration #5:
## Do you eat when you are stressed out?

If so, this is an emotional hunger which can also be triggered if you are bored, upset, or tired. If it is physical hunger, the Mediterranean Diet Plan will be exactly the answer to the problem. You can fill up on the fiber-filled fruit and veggies. The Med Diet plan will provide the bulk and will still be lower in calorie content because all the meals are healthy.

## Consideration #6: (This is a Good One!)
## Do you enjoy eating soup regularly?

Research has indicated that soup might keep you full longer. So, by using soup as the starter course of your meal, there is not as much chance of you over-eating.

For example, if you have some veggies and chicken with a full glass of water, you will feel full for quite some time after. On the other hand, if you consider changing the way you prepare the meal, use the water to make soup instead which not only tastes better, it will provide the same full and satisfied feeling. It is somewhat of a mind game with your body.

The reasoning behind this is that your stomach will empty more slowly if you consume the soup as one unit instead of having the chicken and veggies and a drink of water as an individual unit. The final result is that your stomach wall is stretched out for longer periods of time, which will send a message to your brain to feel less hunger for longer spans of time.

### Generalized Shopping Basics

You have seen numerous items discussed in each of the Mediterranean meals. This will provide you with a reminder list for your shopping convenience:

### Fruits:

- Melons
- Pineapple

- Apricots
- Strawberries
- Applesauce
- Cherries
- Nectarines
- Figs
- Dates
- Bananas
- Peaches
- Pears
- Mango
- Grapes
- Apples

## Poultry and Eggs:

Duck, chicken, guinea fowl

## Dairy Products:

- Plain yogurt
- Fat-free sour cream or fat-free half-n-half
- Shredded strong cheeses (ex. Asiago, ricotta, brie, feta, etc.)
- Fat-free milk, hemp or rice milk, soy milk, or almond milk

## Lean Protein:

- Nuts like dry-roasted and unsalted almonds, pistachios, nut butter, and walnuts
- Egg Substitutes
- Shellfish/Fish: Halibut, tuna, salmon, flounder, shrimp, eel, crab, lobster, mackerel, octopus, sardines, squid, yellowtail, abalone, sea bass
- Peas, beans, and lentils; frozen with no additives or canned if rinsed
- Vegetarian Proteins: Tempeh, tofu, etc.

## Fats and Oils:

- Spray oils
- Canola oil

- Extra-virgin olive oil (EVOO)

## Seasonings and Spices:

- Anise
- Bay Leaf
- Chiles
- Clove
- Cumin
- Capers
- Fresh Herbs: Dill rosemary, basil, parsley, mint, etc.
- Mustards
- Whole or minced garlic
- Horseradish
- Aged balsamic vinegar
- Lime, lemon
- Pepper
- Thyme
- Tarragon
- Many other low-sodium blends or seasonings

## Vegetables and Tubers:

- Artichokes
- Asparagus
- Beets
- Brussels Sprouts
- Celery
- Collards
- Chicory
- Cucumbers
- Carrots
- Dark Green Veggies
- Roasted Bell Peppers
- Broccoli
- Cabbage
- Peas
- Potatoes
- Sweet Potatoes
- Pumpkin
- Purslane

- Radishes
- Rutabaga
- Eggplant
- Spinach
- Turnips
- Zucchini
- Onions (red, white, sweet), chives, shallots
- Tomatoes

## One Final Word: Snacks

By now; you have gotten the Mediterranean idea for meal preparation. Now it is time to discover what to do about the snacks in between those carefully planned meals. It is essential to consume healthy foods at snack time to keep your diet balanced. Remember, don't eat unless you are hungry! Consider these treats for midmorning or midafternoon treats. If you have a late dinner, you could also enjoy a few indulgences until dinner; only a few though.

According to *Everyday Health*, a healthy snack is considered within the limits of 150 to 200 calories daily. The snack is intended to keep a stable blood sugar level and ward off the major food cravings.

- **Fruit & Greek Yogurt:** This protein-rich snack doesn't actually come from Greece today, but it's so good. Top the healthy yogurt off with some sunflower seeds, a handful of your favorite berries, and a drizzle of honey. Yummy!
- **Dried Fruit & Nuts:** Combine your favorite nuts with some mixed berries or dried cherries to get a protein boost that's full of heart-healthy omega-3 fatty acids.
- **Figs or Dates**: These two are key elements of the Mediterranean diet and grow well in the Mediterranean region. You can pack them as a simple snack if you are on-the-go and cannot prepare anything else. How great is that?
- **Hummus & Pita**: You cannot get much more Mediterranean than with the hummus made from chickpeas and sesame paste/tahini. You can prepare your own without additional preservatives. Spread a few tablespoons over the pita and enjoy the snack.
- **Kalamata Olives:** The brine flavor of this simple snack plays a major role against the olive's natural oil. The olives contain

antioxidants including oleic acid, hydroxytyrosol, and tyrosol. Garnish with a little feta cheese for a tasty combo.

- **Tuna Salad & Crackers**: Have a can of oil-packed tuna with a splash of red wine vinegar, scallions, and a squeeze of mustard. Have some whole wheat crackers when the urge strikes.
- **Fruit Slices & Your Nut Butter**: Choose either heart-healthy option of cashew or almond butter and dip some apples or pears into them for a sweet tooth surprise. Make your own almond butter by roasting and blending raw almonds. Have some healthy fats, fiber, and protein!
- **Tomato & Feta Cheese**: Choose a ripened summer tomato when you have those hunger pains. Slice and drizzle the tomato with oil and a couple sprigs of basil. A bit of fresh mozzarella cheese is a tasty topping to enjoy any time.
- **Sun-Dried Tomato & Goat Cheese Spread**: The tomatoes are rich in lycopene, calcium iron, as well as Vitamin A & C. Since they're packaged with oil, you are also getting a heart-healthy boost. Smear a layer of goat cheese over a whole wheat cracker and garnish it with the tomatoes. Add a basil leaf and enjoy.

# Conclusion

I hope you have enjoyed your copy of *Mediterranean Meal Prep: Complete Beginner's Guide to Save Time and Eat Healthier with Batch Cooking For The Mediterranean Diet*. Let's hope it was informative and provided you with all of the tools you need to achieve your goals of preparing healthy meals and saving tons of time.

The next step is to recall the essential foods that you will be using for meal preparation with the Mediterranean diet plan. By investing in quality preparation aids, you won't need to spend that much money once the preparation wheels are rolling. Start by making a list!

This is a general list of some of the items you should consider stocking in your kitchen.

## Dairy and Cheese
- Greek Yogurt
- Eggs
- Cheese of your choice

## Frozen Products
- Vegetables of your choice
- Shrimp
- Berries

## Healthy Fats
- Avocados
- Extra-virgin olive oil (EVOO)
- Favorite Seeds and nuts

## Legumes and Canned Beans
- Lentils
- Garbanzo
- Black
- White
- Kidney

## Meat and Seafood
- Lean Pork
- Chicken
- Salmon

## Whole Grains
- Quinoa
- Whole Grain Pasta
- Farro

## Unlimited—Your Favorites
- Fresh Vegetables
- Herbs
- Spices

The next step is to decide how dedicated you are to the process. You can begin small to see how well you can adjust to the methods used in successful meal preparation. Make a list of the food items which are your favorites and make a shopping list.

You can go big and use a spreadsheet to lay out the weekly or monthly menus. Each of the recipes provides you with the information needed to keep your refrigerator and freezer stocked with tasty food whenever you are hungry.

As a reminder, these are some of the benefits you will have if you choose the Mediterranean style of eating for a lifetime:

- Lowered Cholesterol
- Lowered Blood Pressure
- Improved Blood Sugar Levels
- Weight Loss
- Stronger Immune System: Get sick less often
- Healthier and more radiant nails, skin, and hair.

- Less muscle pain or soreness
- More body strength

Finally, if you found this book useful in any way, a review on Amazon is always appreciated!

# Recipes Index In Alphabetical Order

# Other Books By Elizabeth Wells

**Mediterranean Diet For Beginners**
The Complete Guide To Lose Weight And Live Healthier Following
The Mediterranean Lifestyle

The Mediterranean Diet has been voted by many scientists as one of the healthiest diets in the world. The pure reality of this diet plan is that it isn't something to be considered as a short-term fad diet plan. It is a lifestyle that is loaded with healthy habits, great food, and a substantial amount of benefits, and it has been proven to help lose weight faster and achieve several other benefits like lower risk of heart disease and decreased risk of type 2 diabetes.

The Mediterranean Diet is based on the eating habits of people living in the Mediterranean region, and includes relatively high consumption of olive oil, vegetables and fruits and moderate consumption of fish, cheese, yogurt and other dairy products.

In this book you'll learn everything you need to know to lose weight, improve your overall health and experience the countless benefits of the Mediterranean lifestyle.

**The Mediterranean Diet For Beginners Will Teach You:**
- The Basics Of The Mediterranean Diet Plan
- How To Lose Weight The Mediterranean Way
- 11 Health Benefits You'll Get By Following The Mediterranean Lifestyle
- What You Should Eat And Drink - Explained
- How To Eat The Right Amounts Of Servings Using The Mediterranean Pyramid
- 5 Unhealthy Food Groups To Avoid
- A Complete 14-day Mediterranean Meal Plan
- 3 Healthy Alternatives To Common Unhealthy Foods
- Tips And Tricks For Eating Healthy Even When Eating Out
- A List Of Healthier (And Delicious) Choices To Order At The Most Famous Restaurants
- 60+ Mediterranean Diet Recipes For Tasty Breakfasts, Lunches, Sides, Dinners, Desserts, Snacks, Smoothies And Sauces
- And Much, Much More

And remember, the Mediterranean diet is not a restrictive eating style and even embraces food such as eggs, cheese, meat and some sweets – just in small amounts to savor and enjoy. The secret is to do as the Mediterranean people have done for centuries: eat healthy food, get walking and make exercise a part of your healthy routine, and if the moment comes, don't be leery of opening that bottle of rich cabernet you have been savoring for special occasions.

**Some Mediterranean Diet Recipes You'll Find Inside The Book:**
- Bento Lunchtime Delight
- Mediterranean Chicken Quinoa Bowl
- Mediterranean Tuna Antipasto Salad
- Greek Egg Frittata
- Herbed Mashed Potatoes with Greek Yogurt
- Marinated Olives & Feta
- Picnic Snack
- Hassel-back Caprese Chicken

- Salmon Rice Bowl
- Shrimp Scampi
- Cucumber Roll-Ups
- Cherries – Toasted Almonds and Ricotta

**Enjoy your new lifestyle today!**

**"Mediterranean Diet For Beginners" by Elizabeth Wells is available at Amazon.**

**Mediterranean Diet**
Step-by-Step Guide for Beginners to Eat Well and Stay Healthy the
Mediterranean Way

The Mediterranean diet is based on a variety of cuisine options rich
in aromas, nutrients, and colors. It has been voted by many scientists
as one of the healthiest diets in the world.

The Mediterranean lifestyle comes from the eating habits of people
who live in Italy and Greece, it is not a restrictive diet. This is
important because often people hear the word "diet" and
automatically think they will have to abandon all their favourite foods.
One of the best things about the Mediterranean diet is that it is so
varied, and it isn't restrictive at all. You will eat healthier while still
enjoying what you love.

In this book you'll learn what the Mediterranean diet is and how to
follow it to lose weight, improve your health and experience the
countless benefits of the Mediterranean lifestyle.

You will discover how to make the transition to this healthier lifestyle in a way that is smooth and easy. Usually people fail to eat healthier because they can't stick to their new healthy habits, that's why this guide includes a 30-day meal plan with easy to make recipes that will help you eat healthier.

## This Guide Will Teach You:
- The History And Basics Of The Mediterranean Diet Plan
- All The Foods You Should And Shouldn't Eat
- How To Easily Transition To The Mediterranean Diet
- 13 Tips To Enjoy All The Benefits Of The Mediterranean Lifestyle
- How To Make Lifestyle Changes In A Smooth Way
- All The Health Benefits You'll Get By Following The Mediterranean Diet
- How To Eat The Right Nutrients With The Mediterranean Pyramid
- A Complete 30-Day Mediterranean Meal Plan
- Easy To Make Recipes For Healthy Breakfasts, Lunches, And Dinners
- And Much, Much More

Remember, the secret is to do what the Mediterranean people have been doing for centuries: eat healthy foods, have an active lifestyle, and if the moment comes, don't be leery of opening that bottle of rich cabernet you have been savoring for special occasions.

## Some Mediterranean Diet Recipes You'll Find In This Book:
- Breakfast Quinoa
- Cauliflower and Kale Frittata
- Egg Salad Sandwich
- White Bean and Chicken Soup
- Spaghetti Squash Lasagna
- Grilled Polenta with Vegetables
- Artichoke and Tomato Gnocchi
- Caprese Chicken
- Pepperoni and Brussels Sprouts Pizza
- Shrimp Piccata

## Make a healthy choice today!

## "Mediterranean Diet" by Elizabeth Wells is available at Amazon.

Made in the USA
Lexington, KY
21 November 2018